A Friend Like Iggy

Written by Kathryn Cole 🐾 Photography by Ian Richards

Second Story Press

If you are like me, you don't say much to people you've just met, especially when they ask you a lot of questions.

If you are like me, you don't especially want to go to the doctor, even when you know the doctor is nice.

If you are like me, you'd really rather not
speak in front of a roomful of strangers.
And if you are like me, you really, really
don't want certain people there while
you are telling what happened to you.
Even if the things you have to say are true,
and everyone says they are important.

That might make you sad and angry, or
afraid and confused, even though it's okay to
have all of those feelings, and even though
what happened was not your fault.

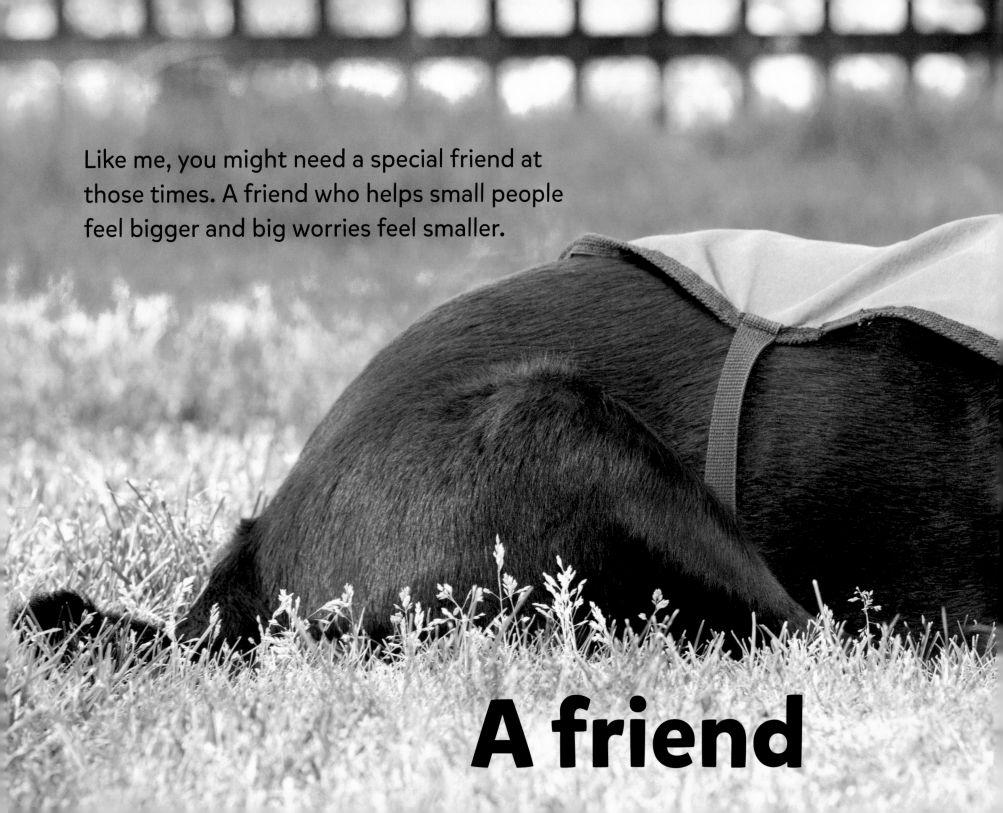

Like me, you might need a special friend at those times. A friend who helps small people feel bigger and big worries feel smaller.

A friend

like Iggy!

I didn't know what to expect as I rode the
elevator up to my first visit at the center.
I sure didn't expect a large black dog with a
gentle face. But there was Iggy, sitting beside
a smiling woman, waiting patiently—just for me!

His big brown eyes seemed to say
"Don't worry. I come here every day and
I like this place." If Iggy could be calm here,
so could I. The butterflies that had been
fluttering in my stomach went to sleep.

The woman's name was Maggie. She was Iggy's
handler, the person who looks after him.
She gave him permission to move "forward."
Iggy stood right away, picked up one of his toys,
and brought it to me. Together we entered an office.

I sat down, feeling better already, and when Iggy
was told to "visit," he came and put his big head
in my lap. I patted him as I listened and answered
questions. Iggy's coat was as smooth and shiny
as silk. My hand slid easily over his soft ears and
words slipped out of my mouth, just as easily.
Before I knew it, my first meeting was over.

"See you next week," Maggie said.

"Will Iggy be here when I come back?" I asked.

"Of course," she said. "That's his job. He's trained as an accredited facility dog. That means he helps us relax and work together."

Just then, Iggy plopped down and rolled onto his back. "Right now, he's not thinking about work," Maggie told me, shaking her head. "He's asking for a tummy rub."

That made me laugh. I squatted down and rubbed his tummy. "Thanks for being here, Iggy. See you next time."

The next time, and all the times after that, Iggy was there.

He was with me when I spoke to the police officer and told her what happened.

He was there when I went to the doctor.

If I sat on the floor, Iggy would lie across my legs like a warm, cozy blanket.

If I was drawing pictures, he would lie beside me and watch.

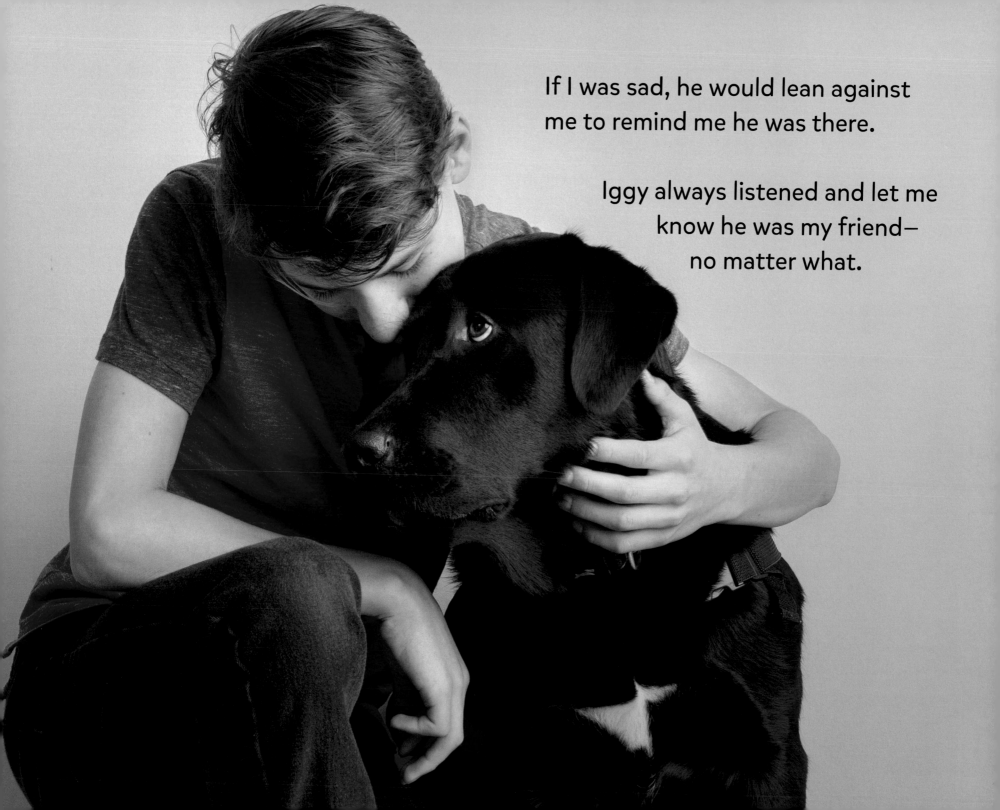

If I was sad, he would lean against me to remind me he was there.

Iggy always listened and let me know he was my friend—no matter what.

One day, after many visits and talks, I had a very important job to do. I needed to go to a place called court and tell what happened to me. Other people would talk about what they knew. All I had to do was tell the truth and say if I didn't know or couldn't remember something. But that isn't as easy as it sounds.

For the first time in a long time, the butterflies in my stomach were back.

The courtroom was large, and I had to remember to use my big voice so everyone could hear. Most of the people there were strangers. A few were friends. And there was someone else. It was the person I didn't want to see or talk in front of. That's when Iggy helped most of all.

He came to be with me in court and he was allowed to sit right beside me. Maggie said I could keep my hand on him while I spoke. But just having him close helped me to be brave. Iggy always made my job easier and he did it again that day. He was a first-class, fabulous...facility dog!

When we were finished we celebrated a job well done.
I had a cookie with pink icing. Iggy really wanted a
cookie too, but he isn't allowed people food, so he
waited patiently. Then we played in the park!

What a relief! I had been brave and honest.
I said exactly what I meant to say.
I did my job in court, and Iggy helped me.

After the court day I made a few more trips to the center, but the time finally came for the last visit. I was proud of myself and happy that I didn't need to come anymore. Still, it was hard to leave everyone who had been so nice to me.

I knew I would miss Iggy most of all. But there were
other kids who needed him now. Maggie gave me a
card with his picture on it so I could look at it any time I
wanted. Iggy is a superstar. He has his own business card!
Maggie also told me I could follow him on Instagram!

Iggy's tail wagged when I hugged him good-bye.
"Keep up the good work, Iggy," I whispered in his ear.
"Remember me...."

I
will
always
remember
you!

Boost Child & Youth Advocacy Centre (Boost CYAC) is an innovative community response to child abuse investigations in Toronto, Ontario. A partnership between community and government agencies, it brings together all professionals involved in child abuse cases under one roof, for a coordinated, interdisciplinary response to child abuse. In addition to housing Toronto's only child and youth advocacy center, Boost CYAC offers a number of direct services including primary prevention, public education, advocacy, and support during and after the investigation, trauma assessment, therapy, and court preparation for child witnesses.

The BARK Program at Boost CYAC provides additional support to children and youth through the use of accredited facility dogs. These dogs are specially trained to help keep children and youth calm and centered during what can be a stressful and difficult experience. Boost CYAC has two facility dogs; Iggy, whom you have just read about in this story, and Jersey, who works at one of our other locations. Iggy and Jersey both provide comfort and support to children and youth in the forensic interview, the medical examination, counselling, court preparation sessions, and while testifying in court.

Iggy was bred, raised, and trained by National Service Dogs (NSD) in Cambridge, Ontario and was born on March 23, 2015. The puppies from NSD live with "puppy raisers" and are trained for two years before going to work.

Iggy works at Boost CYAC five days a week, but at night and on the weekends he goes home with his primary handler. At home, Iggy doesn't wear his working vest. He gets to play with other dogs and cuddle with his family, just like a regular dog. Iggy has been so helpful that Boost CYAC is getting another facility dog. Soon he will have a new canine co-worker join him at Boost CYAC!

You can follow Iggy and Jersey on Instagram at @BoostforKidsIggy and @BoostforKidsJersey.